Writing Frameworks

Writing Frameworks

Easy-to-use structures
for creating confident,
successful writers

David Whitehead

Pembroke Publishers Limited

© 2003 User Friendly Resource Enterprises Ltd.

Pembroke Publishers
538 Hood Road
Markham, Ontario, Canada L3R 3K9
www.pembrokepublishers.com

Distributed in the U.S. by Stenhouse Publishers
477 Congress Street
Portland, ME 04101
www.stenhouse.com

This edition is adapted from *Writing Frameworks* originally published by User Friendly
Resource Enterprises Ltd. in New Zealand in 1997.

National Library of Canada Cataloguing in Publication

Whitehead, David
    Writing frameworks : easy-to-use structures for creating confident,
successful writers in all genres / David Whitehead. — 1st Canadian ed.

Includes index.
ISBN 1-55138-154-0

    1. English language—Composition and exercises—Study and teaching
(Elementary). I. Title.

LB1576.W4863 2003   372.62'3   C2002-906051-6

Editor: Pauline Scanlan, Kathryn Cole, Ann Manson
Cover Design: John Zehethofer
Layout Design: Adrienne Clemens, JayTee Graphics
Illustrations: Geraldine Sloane

Printed and bound in Canada
9 8 7 6 5 4 3 2 1

Contents

Introduction

The exercises in this book involve factual writing that not only deals with a student's school life, but the world beyond. The writing frameworks will help students develop important skills in writing reports, explaining a procedure, describing an event, and recounting details. In this kind of functional writing the audience is important and the writer needs to make connections between the text and the target audience. Functional writing also demands a greater attention to purpose, context, content, organization, unity, and coherence than "literary writing."

Students will encounter this kind of writing throughout their "professional" lives. At some time or other they will probably have to write a resumé and covering letter when they apply for a job. Writing letters and reports, recounting details, and providing written analyses of data with explanations and recommendations are also part of most jobs. And many jobs involve a lot of writing — from writing brochures, advertising, and manuals to writing letters and speeches.

The frameworks in this book will help students build skills in this kind of factual writing. They will learn to consider the needs of their audience and organize writing that is brief, to the point, and makes sense to the target audience.

What Are Writing Frameworks?

Writing frameworks have been designed to help students think, before they write, in ways that will help them to compose factual, nonfiction texts — a writing genre that many students find difficult.

There are two types of writing frameworks in this resource:

- frameworks which help the **prewriting** of texts
- frameworks which help the **draft writing** of texts.

Each **prewriting framework** is linked to a **draft writing** framework. For example, the Brainstorm prewriting framework helps students record and organize information before they draft a Report; and the Perspective prewriting framework helps students to think about two or more sides of an issue before they draft a Discussion.

The frameworks for writing drafts reflect the linguistic conventions, or generally accepted structures, of a specific type of factual genre. For example, the Report draft writing framework helps students to write topical paragraphs, and prompts them to use subheadings.

How Do You Use Writing Frameworks?

Frameworks are not designed to restrict either literacy or creativity. Rather, they are designed as supportive prewriting and draft writing aids. Once students understand the prewriting strategies and the way the conventions of various factual texts can be combined, teachers can dispense with the frameworks altogether.

Teachers might choose to model the two types of writing frameworks with the whole class first. After that, students could practise in groups before accepting the challenge of using them independently.

Some writing frameworks require gradual introduction. For example, the Brainstorm framework will probably require five or more sessions. The Brainstorm lessons will progressively demonstrate how to:

- collect
- label
- design questions
- identify resources to answer questions.

Likewise, the three Argument frameworks, on pages *51* through *58*, and the Report framework, on page *39*, are complex and need to be gradually introduced over several weeks.

In the same way the Characteristics Grid needs gradual introduction. For example, teachers might first ask students to complete a prepared grid with labels and descriptors. Later, students might list the descriptors, and much later, while researching, record labels and descriptors onto a blank grid. Finally, teachers might demonstrate how students can use patterns among the data to write summary statements.

Why Use Writing Frameworks?

The **draft writing frameworks** are designed to help students achieve confidence in their writing. The **prewriting frameworks** are designed to help students with *processing information* and *thinking critically*.

In this way the frameworks assist students to develop their:

- knowledge of language
- knowledge of thinking strategies
- knowledge of the writing process.

The Importance of Modelling

Underpinning the use of the frameworks is a belief that students may never acquire sufficient knowledge about language or knowledge of prewriting strategies without modelling.

Such modelling is also consistent with the beliefs that underpin a balanced literacy classroom, but only if the knowledge about language and strategies is acquired in meaningful, purposeful, and authentic student-centred contexts, and after students have built up their knowledge of a topic.

When Do You Use Writing Frameworks?

An understanding of language development and the needs of their students will assist teachers to determine when they might use the various frameworks. It may be that younger students prefer to write Recounts and that older students have a preference for writing Arguments and Discussions. Recounting a recent concrete experience may be a less intellectually demanding task than arguing an abstract belief. Of course, students in the early years should have opportunities to write and talk in different forms — even a five-year-old can argue! But teachers may feel that there is a different emphasis in the types of writing students do at various ages.

The use of writing frameworks might also link to various curriculum areas through the year. For example, observational drawings as an art and science topic might be linked to the writing of Descriptions. The reading of biography in social studies might be linked to the writing of a Recount, and a health education topic might result in students writing Explanations.

How to Use this Resource

This book provides:
- prewriting strategies and associated frameworks
- models of Recount, Procedure, Description, Report, Explanation, Argument, and Discussion texts
- draft writing frameworks for each of the above forms
- assessment record sheets.

Teachers are encouraged to use the resource flexibly to meet the needs of their students and the curriculum. For example, more experienced writers may not need draft writing frameworks but they may need to acquire some of the prewriting strategies.

The most important thing is that you make the resource work for you and the students in your class.

David Whitehead

Recount

Using Timelines and Excitement Graphs

Recounts are time-sequenced. A **Timeline** helps students to work out the sequence of events they wish to recount. It allows them to indicate at what time (*that morning, after, later that night*) the main events occurred, and describe these events using words against each time signal on the timeline. In short, timelines help students to organize their recounts and make time links between and among events.

> ▌ *Timelines help students to organize their recounts.*

One approach to the construction of a timeline is to have students write the main events of an experience or historical text onto card strips, then sequence them in time order. Then they might decide how to show when the events took place.

On Monday I took my pet rabbit to school and ...

The next day my class drew pictures of all the animals that had ...

On Thursday we had a visit from Jill, a vet, who ...

By the weekend I had almost finished my "pet" project ready for ...

Alternatively, students could decide on the main events, represent these as paintings or drawings, then sequence them in time order in the form of a spectacular wall display. Captions and speech bubbles could be added later.

Excitement Graphs can be added to timelines to provide another dimension. One axis of the graph represents "time" like a timeline, the other axis "excitement." A line graph joining the events provides a graphic representation of any climax in the recount.

> ▌ *Excitement graphs present a visual record of climaxes in the recount.*

Timelines with key dates also provide a useful study guide for readers. As students encounter the dates in the text they add, in summary form, the main event that occurred on that date.

Timeline

Time/Date	What Happened

Excitement Graph

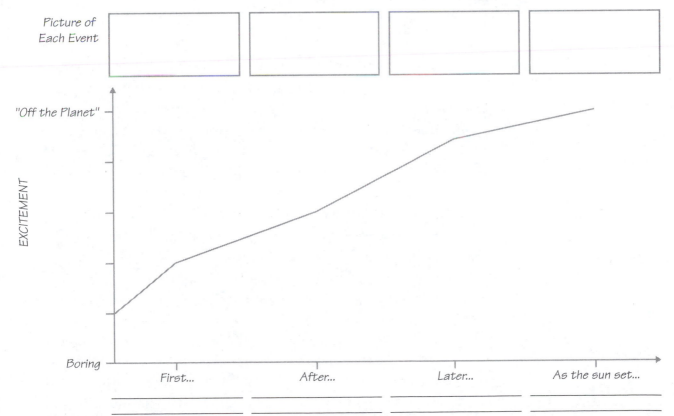

Picture of Each Event

"Off the Planet"

EXCITEMENT

Boring

First...   After...   Later...   As the sun set...

Summary of Each Event
TIME

Using a News Telling Framework

The "Morning Talk", a form of Recount, is an institution in most primary schools. These talks contrast with the "Show and Tell" talks that usually involve description rather than recount.

Morning talks usually recount a recent event of importance to the speaker. The **Telling the News Framework** on the next page assists speakers to include all the components usually required in these talks, that is, the **when, where, why, what, how,** and **who** of an event.

Typically, as part of the morning talk lesson, teachers will form students into co-operative learning buzz groups of four to six, with each student given the responsibility of sharing a piece of news. The Telling The News Framework, which can be used before and as students share their news, reminds them of the components of their talk.

■ *The News Telling Framework acts as a prompt sheet.*

If one student from each buzz group is chosen to share their news with the rest of the class, they might record notes for the talk on the Telling The News Framework and use it as a prompt during their presentation. Alternatively, if students are asked to write their news in diaries, these frameworks can be used to help draft their written texts.

Using an Event Framework

The **Thinking About an Event Framework**, used in conjunction with the Telling The News Framework, adds a critical dimension to a morning talk, by providing students with ways of thinking critically about an event reported in the newspaper or in a history text.

■ *The Event Framework helps students to think critically.*

Typically, the teacher will use the questions on this framework as a teaching prompt with younger students. But by age eight or so, students should choose one or more questions and apply them to the recount they are reading or constructing.

Because the Thinking About An Event Framework introduces a critical dimension, it provides an introduction to Argument and Discussion writing.

Telling the News

- **What is the topic of the news you are going to think about?**

  _____

- **When:** When did it happen?

  _____

  _____

- **Who:** Who created the news?

  _____

  _____

- **Where:** Where did the news happen?

  _____

  _____

  _____

- **What:** What happened?

  _____

  _____

  _____

  _____

- **Why:** Why did it happen?

  _____

  _____

  _____

  _____

Thinking About an Event

- **What is the event you are going to think about?**

  _____

- **OK:** Was it OK for this event to happen in our lifetime or in the past? Will it be OK for this event to happen again in the future?

  _____

  _____

  _____

- **Needed:** Was the event, or the thing that happened, needed?

  _____

  _____

  _____

- **Achieve:** Did the event, or thing that happened, achieve its purpose?

  _____

  _____

  _____

- **Learn:** What can we learn from what happened?

  _____

  _____

  _____

  _____

- **Change:** How and why would you change what happened?

  _____

  _____

  _____

14

Recounting an Event

STAR SWIMMER FROM SPORTING FAMILY

WHO, WHAT, WHEN, WHERE
Students who went to the school swimming sports championship on Saturday February 15th at the David Snow Pool saw a star of the future.

EVENT ONE
Statement
Tania Weintrop, from Hamilton Secondary, came first in the 200m backstroke, 200m butterfly and the 100m breaststroke events.
Description
Weintrop broke her personal best times in the backstroke and butterfly, beating her greatest rival, Jody Kennedy, from Westmount Secondary.
Comment
This 13-year-old athlete from a well-known sporting family is set to become one of the fastest swimmers in the city for the under 16 age group.

EVENT TWO	EVENT THREE	
Statement	Statement	Further information about the
Description	Description	championships would be ex-
Comment	Comment	panded in two more paragraphs

CONCLUSION
With help from Tania Weintrop, Hamilton Secondary stood first as the school with the most points on the day. Second and third school placings were taken by Westmount Secondary and Elmwood High School.
Comment
If these championship are anything to go by we can look forward to some possible medal prospects from the schools for the Pan Pacific Games in two years' time.

Writing a Recount

A Recount tells what happened. If you are going to write a Recount about something you did, use the words "I" or "we". If you are going to write a Recount about what someone else did, use the words "he", "she", or "they".

Title

- The title of my Recount is:

_____

Paragraph One

- Write a paragraph that says **who** took part in the event, **when** and **where** the event took place, and **why** and **how** the event took place.

_____

_____

_____

_____

_____

_____

_____

Event One

- Write about the first thing that happened, and use the past tense. Start by saying what happened, and then add your comment (your own thoughts). Useful words are: **first, then, next, after that, finally, later, the next day.**

_____

_____

_____

_____

_____

_____

_____

Writing a Recount

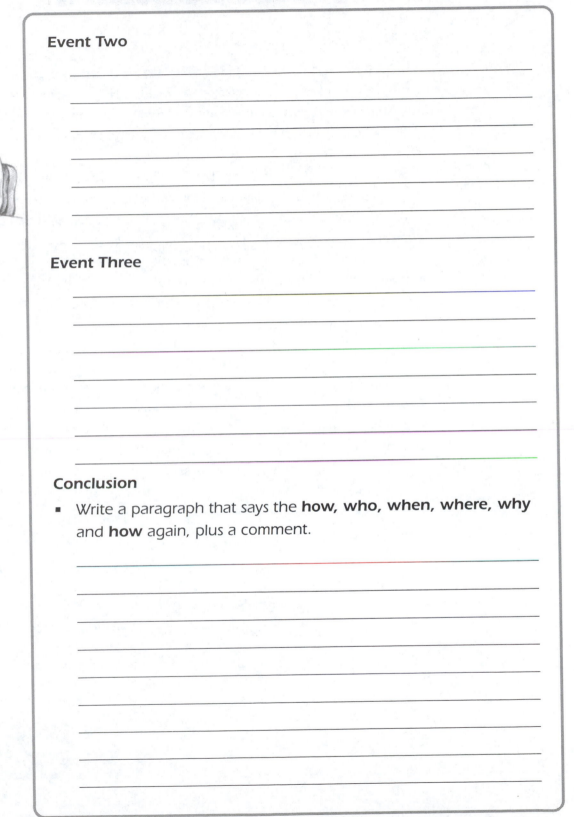

Event Two

_____

_____

_____

_____

_____

_____

_____

Event Three

_____

_____

_____

_____

_____

_____

_____

Conclusion

- Write a paragraph that says the **how, who, when, where, why** and **how** again, plus a comment.

_____

_____

_____

_____

_____

_____

_____

_____

Procedure

How to Use a Flow Chart

The boxes on the following **Flow Chart Framework** can be used to record, in written and visual form, each step of a Procedure. The completion of this requires that students first work out the number of steps in the Procedure and then draw sufficient boxes. Between the arrows that separate the boxes students can insert the step links, for example: **After..., Next..., Finally....**

Teachers may choose to divide the class into groups sufficient to cover all the steps in a Procedure. This approach requires consensus among the group about what will be written or drawn in the boxes. The approach also ensures that expertise is pooled.

The ultimate test of any Procedure is that someone else can successfully follow it. Writing a clear, accurate Procedure is difficult. Even students experienced with narrative writing, where much is inferred, find difficulty realizing that a reader may not have the same background knowledge of the procedure as they do. Therefore, each step in the Procedure must be "consumer tested" to see that sufficient has been said.

Frequently, Procedures use both diagrams and written text to make things clear. Provide students with numerous models and discuss how these are set out.

Students might begin by first writing a simple Procedure, such as how to put the top on a bottle, but even this is tricky. Perhaps students could first rehearse this Procedure in pairs, with one student providing the instructions and the other carrying them out "to-the-letter", then later they might jointly work on their written text.

■ *The Flow Chart Framework records, in written and visual form, the steps in a procedure.*

■ *Each step in a written procedure needs to be "consumer tested".*

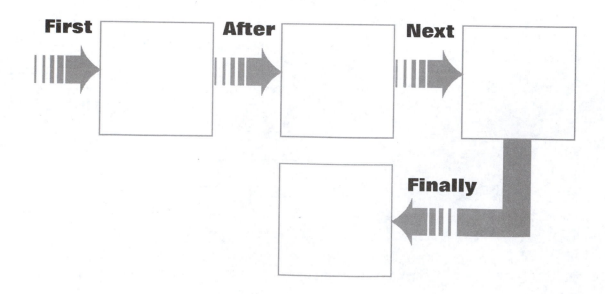

Using a Flow Chart Framework

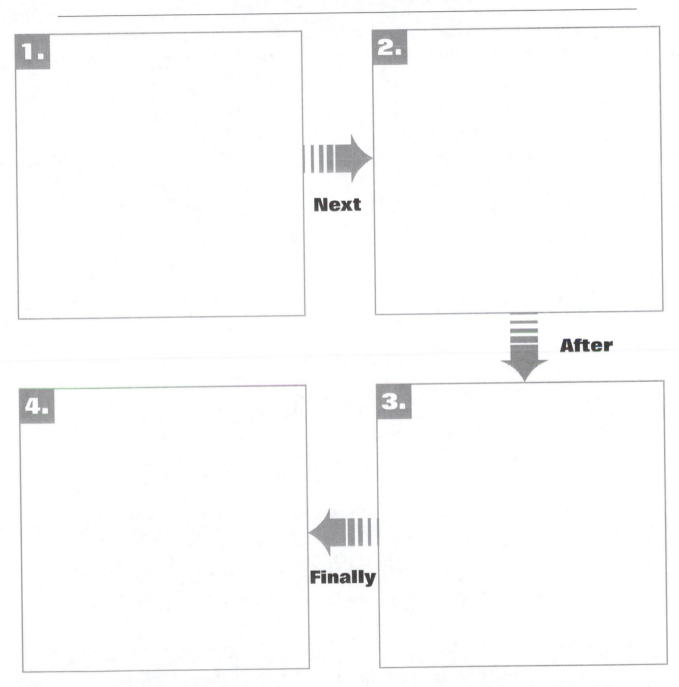

Use this sheet to either draw a picture, or write instructions for a simple Procedure that you want someone to follow. Then design your own flow chart for more complicated Procedures that have more steps.

19

PROCEDURE
Text Model

Writing a Procedure

HOW TO MAKE OYSTER SOUP

INTRODUCTION

Serving oyster soup is a yummy way to begin a special winter meal. Use fresh or thawed frozen oysters for this soup. To get the best flavour, make the soup before you need it, let it cool, then reheat without boiling just before you serve it.

BODY

Ingredients

For 4-6 servings you will need:

18 oysters

1-2 cloves of garlic

a little grated nutmeg

75g of butter

6 Tbsp flour

4-5 cups of milk

juice of one lemon

salt and pepper

Method

First, drain the oysters and keep the liquid. **Second,** cut the fleshy part of the oyster from the beard (the frilly part around the "meaty" eye). **Next,** crush the garlic, then cook the beards in butter with garlic and nutmeg for 3-4 minutes without browning. **Then,** stir in flour and cook 2 minutes longer. **Now,** stir in the oyster liquid and 1 cup of milk. When thick add another 2 cups. When the mixture has boiled chop it up in the food processor, then separate the beards using a sieve. **Finally,** add the oyster flesh, lemon juice, and extra milk.

CONCLUSION

Don't boil after adding the oyster flesh. Serve with fingers of toast.

Don't keep the soup in the fridge for more than a day. Eat and enjoy!

Writing a Procedure

A Procedure tells us how to do something, such as change a bicycle tire. Some Procedures are called "instructions", others "directions".

Title

- The title of my Procedure is:

_____

Introduction

- Write a paragraph that says what Procedure you are going to describe. Say it in a way that invites us to read on.

_____

_____

_____

Body

- Describe steps in the Procedure.
  Show each step by using: 1, 2, 3....., or **first, second, next, finally.** You might put each new step in from the margin.

_____

_____

_____

_____

_____

Conclusion

- Write a paragraph that lets the reader know something special about the Procedure.

_____

_____

_____

_____

21

Description

How to Use Descriptor Frameworks

The **Descriptor Framework** assists students to research and write draft Observation, Description, and Report texts. Each of the six descriptors on the Framework prompt students to think about objects and events in a different way. For example, if the object is a penguin the **Analyze** descriptor might prompt students to describe everything from beak to flippers, and the **Associate** descriptor may prompt the recall of its habitat, food supply, or the use of penguins in advertisements. It probably pays to begin with the **Describe** descriptor, taking care that the students describe rather than compare.

The **Argue** descriptor is likely to elicit critical thinking, especially if students are encouraged to adopt different points of view. For example, a fisherman might argue that penguins are a nuisance, while conservationists argue they are a good thing. Proceed with the other descriptors ensuring that **Comparisons** are made with similar objects, for example penguins and puffins, rather than penguins and automobiles.

Encourage students to record words and phrases on the **Framework** and then write summary sentences based on the three (or so) words in each box that students think are the most important pieces of information they have recorded. Challenge them to come up with the best sentence they can compose that includes these words.

Descriptor Frameworks help students to think about objects and events in different ways.

Descriptor Framework

- **What do you intend to describe?**

  _____

- **Describe:** How does it look, smell, feel, taste, and sound?

  _____

  _____

  _____

  Best sentence:

  _____

  _____

- **Analyze:** What is it made of? What are its parts?

  _____

  _____

  _____

  Best sentence:

  _____

  _____

- **Associate:** What does it make you think of?

  _____

  _____

  _____

  Best sentence:

  _____

  _____

Descriptor Framework

- **Compare:** What is it similar to? What is it different from?

  _____

  _____

  Best sentence:

  _____

  _____

- **Apply:** What can you do with it?

  _____

  _____

  _____

  Best sentence:

  _____

  _____

- **Argue:** Why is this a good thing? Why is this a bad thing?

  _____

  _____

  _____

  Best sentence:

  _____

  _____

Challenge!

How to Play Challenge

Challenge is best used prior to the writing of Descriptions. This prewriting strategy assists students to describe the characteristics of fictional and historical figures, or the characteristics of objects or events. It is designed to help students recall and think about information as they read, listen, or view.

The strategy works best when the number of people, objects, or events is limited to about four. This ensures a manageable task, so that the students are not describing and comparing too many things. Multiple copies of a text are required allowing students to consult the book as they play Challenge. School Journals would be ideal. Students also need small cards on which they print words that describe the characters, objects, or events central to the text, with one word per card. They can work in groups of four.

> ■ *The Challenge game helps students to describe characters, objects, or events.*

Procedure

1. The teacher selects three or four fictional or historical characters from the story/Recount, or a similar number of objects or events from a Description.

2. Each student writes words on their cards that describe the characters, events, or objects as the text is read to, or with them. They do not share their words at this point.

3. Next, groups draw up a grid on a large sheet of paper leaving one space for each character, object, or event.

4. Students take turns placing one card at a time against the character/object/event they feel it best describes, and then justify their placement to the rest of the group. Justification should include referring back to the text.

5. Other students may challenge the placement of a descriptor if they feel it is better placed under another character, or even if it should be removed entirely from the grid.

After all the descriptor cards have been placed on the grid, students might rank them for each character, object, or event with the best descriptor at the top, and words ranked progressively to the least descriptive at the bottom. Students are now well prepared to write their own description.

Describing an Event

HOW HURRICANES AFFECT PEOPLE

Introduction

The introduction lets your readers know the topics your later paragraphs will describe.

> *Pictures of dead and injured people, destroyed homes, and ruined crops remind us of the immediate effects Hurricane Val had on the people of the South Pacific. Val also brought disease as the water of Samoa became contaminated, food shortages as crops rotted in the ground, and a loss of income because of tourists staying away from the damaged island.*

Subheading

Each subheading picks up one of the general statements you wrote in your introduction and gives further explanation and examples.

LOSS OF LIFE AND INJURIES

Statement

Hurricanes brought death to Samoa.

Explanation

People died when buildings in Apia collapsed under the force of the wind and weight of the rain. People drowned as rivers flooded through the valleys and as the sea washed over coastal villages.

Example

Three fishermen from Pau were drowned as they tried to drag their boats up the beach, and a child was drowned when she slipped into a stream swollen by the rain.

Describing an Object

TABBITHA THE CAT

Introduction

The introduction lets your readers know the topics your paragraphs will describe.

Mom's cat, Tabbitha, cannot be described as a pedigree, pure breed cat because her markings and ears are unique, and the way she behaves is sometimes strange.

STATEMENT

Tabbitha has short hair, about 2cm long, with three colors in each hair.

Explanation

These are grey, black, and orange.

Example

Her fur is patterned like a tiger's, except that around the ears and paws it is all black rather than striped.

STATEMENT

Tabbitha has enormous ears.

Example

When she is angry they lie flat down her neck, but most of the time they stick straight up like a jackrabbit's.

STATEMENT

Her favorite past time is hiding in paper bags.

Example

Often I hear a loud purr coming from a bag, but that purr will turn to a "yeow" when Jimmy, Mom's other cat, jumps on the bag. Then Tabbitha leaps out of the bag and across the room as if she was flying.

Writing a Description

Descriptions describe specific things. The focus of a Description is, for example, on one dog, not on all dogs.

INTRODUCTION

- Say something general about the object you are describing. Make it interesting so that readers will want to continue reading.

_____

_____

_____

_____

_____

- Write your first paragraph below. This paragraph should say one thing about the object you are describing. Make a statement, then say a bit more about it and give an example.

_____

_____

_____

_____

_____

- Write another paragraph below. Again, this paragraph should say one thing about the object you are describing. Make a statement, then say a bit more about it and give an example.

_____

_____

_____

_____

_____

Writing a Description

- Write another paragraph below. Again, this paragraph should say one thing about the particular object you are describing. Make a statement, then say a bit more about it and give an example.

_____

_____

_____

_____

CONCLUDING PARAGRAPH

- Describe, in just a few words, the object you are writing about. If you want, you can make a personal comment too.

_____

_____

_____

_____

_____

_____

29

Description and Report

How to Use the Characteristics Grid

Characteristics Grids help students to research and draft Description and Report texts. Specifically, they assist students to record, order, and manipulate information.

The grids provide spaces for the names of characters, objects, or events to be entered across the top, and words describing their characteristics down the side. The sheet should also provide space for summary sentences on the right side and below the grid.

The Characteristics Grids can be scored in two ways. If for example, the words across the top name types of whales, and the characteristics listed down the side describe the features of whales, then the grid is scored by entering checks, crosses, or question marks — the whales either have, or do not have those characteristics, or the students don't yet know. On the other hand, if historical characters are listed across the top and personality characteristics such as "courageous" are listed down the side, then a qualitative 1-5 scale is used to score the framework. Clearly, the qualitative scale is likely to encourage debate.

Characteristics Grids should be gradually introduced. First, teachers should provide a grid complete with labels across the top and descriptors down the side. Students might then complete this after hearing a text read aloud. Note how the descriptors might result from playing **Challenge!** outlined under the Description section of this resource.

Characteristics Grids, complete with labels and descriptors, can also be used by students as reading study guides. Students, individually or in groups, can complete the frameworks as they read, and after reading. At this stage students might be encouraged to add either labels, descriptors, or both to the grids previously prepared by the teacher. Completed grids can be discussed and a consensus reached, although this is not a necessity when frameworks are completed using a 1-5 qualitative scale. What is important is that students substantiate or give reasons for their ratings, and that the class deals with incompletely understood sections of the grid.

After students are confident using the grids, they should be guided to see both vertical and horizontal patterns in the data. These patterns serve as the basis for writing summaries. Encourage students to compare the characteristics of two or more things rather than just summarize the characteristics of a single thing.

Characteristics Grids help students to record, order, and manipulate information.

The Grids are used as an information-gathering tool and a means of making comparisons.

Students have to explain their choices to a small group or the whole class.

Simple Characteristics Grid

LITTLE RED RIDING HOOD

	Wolf	Little Red Riding Hood	Wood Cutter	Grandmother	STATEMENTS
Cunning	5	1	4	1	In some ways the wolf and the woodcutter were similar.
Naive	1	5	1	4	Young children and old people are naive.
Courageous	4	1	5	1	
Feeble	1	3	1	5	

STATEMENTS

While the wolf was cunning and courageous, Grandmother was not.

People who are feeble might also be naive.

KEY

1 = does not have a lot of this characteristic

5 = has lots of this characteristic

Note:

The grid spaces can be divided so that key numbers can be entered to show "beginning of story" and "end of story". For example, Little Red Riding Hood might be very naive at the beginning of the story (5) but less naive at the end (2). Thus 5/2. This makes the grid more complex.

31

Simple Characteristics Grid

WHALES

	Blue whale	Sperm whale	Minke whale	STATEMENTS
Have teeth	X	✓	X	*Only one of the three species has teeth.*
Have baleen	✓	X	✓	
Hunted by Japanese	X	X	✓	*Most whales are not hunted by the Japanese.*

STATEMENTS

In contrast to the Sperm whale, the Blue whale has baleen.

Only the Minke whale is hunted by the Japanese.

KEY

✓ = have

X = do not have

? = we don't know or are unsure

O = some do and some do not

Notes:

- Guide the students to make comparative statements in the news and columns, rather than just listing, for example, that Blue whales do not have teeth, do have baleen and are not hunted by the Japanese.

- A Characteristics Grid completed at the beginning of a topic is likely to have more "?" in the grid.

Complex Characteristics Grid

WHALES

FOOD	Blue whale	Sperm whale	Humpback whale	STATEMENTS
Squid	X	✓	X	
Krill	✓	X	✓	Most of the three whales eat krill.
ANATOMY				
Teeth	X	✓	X	
Baleen	✓	X	✓	
Callosites	X	X	✓	Only humpback whales have callosites.
HABITAT				
Antarctica	✓	?	X	Antarctica is home to the Blue whale.
Pacific	✓	✓	✓	
Off Kaikoura	X	✓	X	

STATEMENTS

Whales with teeth eat squid.

Whales are found throughout the Pacific Ocean.

Only Sperm whales are found off Kaikoura.

KEY

✓ = have

X = do not have

? = we don't know or are unsure

O = some do and some do not

Notes:

The subheadings written in CAPITALS came from the labels of a student brainstorm about whales. The words under each subheading came from the collection and groups of words used in a brainstorm.

Description and Report

How to Use a Brainstorm Framework

The Brainstorm Framework assists students to research and write draft Description and Report texts. There are five parts to the Brainstorm procedure:

- collecting words

- grouping

- labelling

- questioning

- suggesting resources

▨ *The Brainstorm Framework helps students to make links, group, and ask questions.*

Students begin by suggesting words associated with a topic. These words are listed under the heading, **Collection**. When all the words have been listed the teacher asks:

- *"What two words in our collection go together?" to form a group of words (and staying with the student who responded), then asks:*

- *"Why do these two words go together?" then, again staying with the same student asks:*

- *"What are they both about?"*

This last question serves to generate a label for the group of two words.

Next, students can suggest other words that might be included in the group, and other labels that might be used to describe the group. These steps are repeated to form new groups and generate new labels. Note that a word may be used in more than one group and that students are likely to suggest new words that were not included in the original collection.

When the grouping and labelling process is complete, students are prompted to ask three types of questions:

- **questions about words** (given words come from the whole class, some words will be unfamiliar to some students)

▨ *The questioning processes that students move through lead them to further research.*

- **questions about labels** (especially labels above small groups of words, suggesting that little is known about that aspect of the topic)

- **questions that students want answered about the topic.**

Some of these questions might be answered immediately by the class, others may take a whole unit of study to answer, and others may never be answered. Students then suggest resources that may assist them to answer the remaining questions.

Description and Report

As stated on the previous page, the steps in completing a Brainstorm should be introduced gradually. First, the teacher might simply collect words with the students. Later, the teacher may encourage grouping, then labelling. The introduction of questions might coincide with teaching students how to turn titles and subheadings into questions that provide them with a purpose while reading.

When complete, the labels on the Brainstorm provide subheadings, and the groups of words under the labels provide key words for topical paragraphs. Questions raise possibilities for further research and new sections for their factual writing.

Playing Jigsaw

Brainstorm Frameworks can be used in association with the oral language strategy **Jigsaw**. Jigsaw uses labels generated from a Brainstorm to provide topics for a "home" group discussion. The home groups consist of one student per label from the Brainstorm. Then students in each group select one of the labels and join with other students to form expert groups — one expert group per label. These expert groups further investigate their topic.

■ *The Jigsaw strategy helps students to form expert groups.*

It is essential that the teacher provides these groups with additional resource material so that they can further research their "expert" area. Each "expert" group prepares a brief written report on their specialist topic, which all students copy. Then students return to their "home" group to share information.

Note: Students have several options when it comes to organizing what they want to say within their Reports (see the Report Writing Framework.) Some may choose to compare and contrast, for example, in a Report about whales by comparing toothed and baleen species. A second option might be to state a problem and provide a solution. For example, "Whales have been hunted to near extinction. A solution might be to place a ban on whaling." A further option for students might be to use a cause/effect structure, for example, "The demand for whale oil has lead to an increase in hunting."

Brainstorm Model

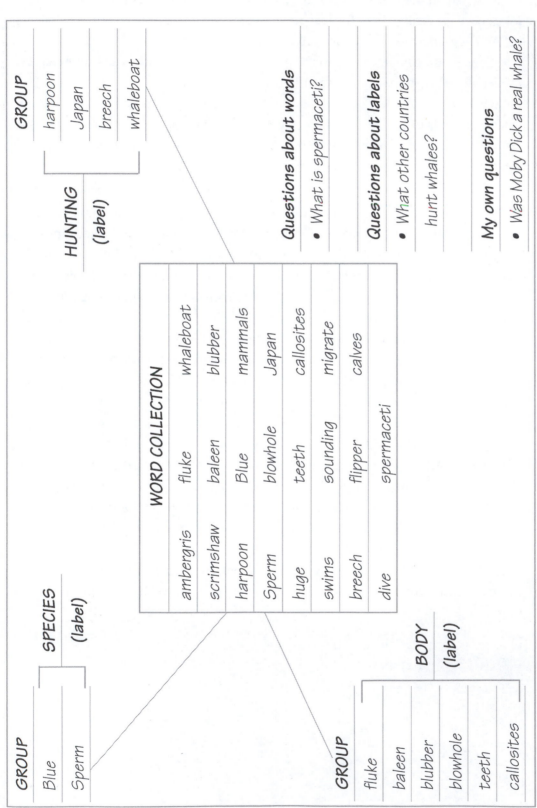

GROUP

harpoon

Japan

breech

whaleboat

HUNTING

(label)

Questions about words

- What is spermaceti?

Questions about labels

- What other countries hunt whales?

My own questions

- Was Moby Dick a real whale?

WORD COLLECTION

ambergris	fluke	whaleboat
scrimshaw	baleen	blubber
harpoon	Blue	mammals
Sperm	blowhole	Japan
huge	teeth	callosites
swims	sounding	migrate
breech	flipper	calves
dive	spermaceti	

SPECIES

(label)

GROUP

Blue

Sperm

BODY

(label)

GROUP

fluke

baleen

blubber

blowhole

teeth

callosites

Organizing a Brainstorm

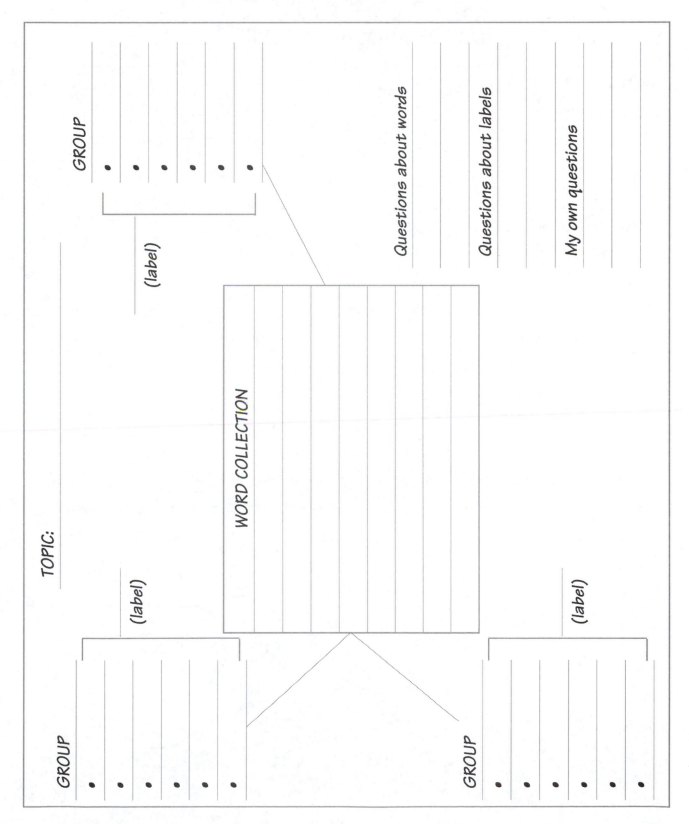

TOPIC:

GROUP

(label)

GROUP

(label)

GROUP

(label)

WORD COLLECTION

Questions about words

Questions about labels

My own questions

Writing a Report

WHALES: MAMMALS OF THE SEA

GENERAL CLASSIFICATION

Whales are mammals (warm blooded creatures) that live in the sea. They belong to the same group of animals as dolphins and porpoise (cetaceans). There are two types of whale: odontoceti (toothed) and mysticeti (baleen).

BODY (Here, two whales are compared)

Subheading: Topic One

appearance

The mouths of toothed and baleen whales are very different. Sperm whales have huge ivory cone-shaped teeth. In contrast, the giant Blue whale has baleen plates instead of teeth. These are like the ridges on the roof of your mouth and feel like your fingernails.

Subheading: Topic Two

feeding

Toothed whales dive for their food, but baleen whales feed on the surface. Some toothed whales dive deep in the ocean and feed upon fish and squid living at the bottom. The sperm whale can dive down more than 1.5 kilometres and feed for an hour at that depth. In contrast, baleen whales eat enormous numbers of small plankton and fish near the surface. The Right whale can skim open mouthed through the water and filter out 1700 kilograms of plankton a day.

Draft Writing Framework

Writing a Report

Reports describe general things. The focus of a Report might be on all dogs, not just on your pet dog.

Title

- The title of my Report is:

_____

General Classification

- Write a General Classification paragraph which says something general about the subject of your Report, for example, a Report about whales might begin by saying: "Whales are big mammals that live in the ocean."

  Remember to interest your readers in the topic.

_____
_____
_____
_____
_____

Body

Subheading

_____

(The subheading tells the reader your topic.)

Paragraph one

- Each paragraph describes something about the topic written under the subheading. Start with a topic sentence, and use the present tense.

_____
_____
_____
_____

© 2003 Writing Frameworks, Pembroke Publishers. Permission to copy for classroom use.

REPORT
*Draft Writing
Framework*

Writing a Report

Paragraph Two

Subheading _____

- Sometimes a Report compares two things.
  For example, "Penguins are like seagulls because they are both
  seabirds, but they are different because they have short wings."

  _____

  _____

  _____

  _____

  _____

  _____

  _____

  _____

  _____

  _____

Paragraph Three

Subheading _____

- Sometimes a Report describes a problem and solution.
  For example, "Seals like to eat penguins, and this is a problem.
  But penguins solve this problem by swimming fast!"

  _____

  _____

  _____

  _____

  _____

  _____

  _____

  _____

  _____

Writing a Report

REPORT

Draft Writing Framework

Paragraph Four

Subheading _____

- Sometimes a Report will say what caused something to happen and the effect. For example, "Seal meat, fur, and oil were in demand during the 1800s. As a result seals were hunted and killed in great numbers."

_____

_____

_____

_____

_____

_____

_____

_____

_____

_____

_____

Explanation

Using the How and Why Sketchboard

The How and Why Sketchboard was designed to help students sort out the cause and effect meanings that are central to any explanation of how or why something occurs. The sketchboard helps in two ways, first by prompting students to represent and expand on what they know verbally and visually, and second by prompting them to make links between the events in the explanation.

Procedure

1. Share ideas and predictions before the investigation; for example, *"I think that things made from metal will not float on water because..."*

2. Outline investigations; for example, *"Try to float this needle on the water."*

3. Share further predictions.

4. Model to students how to use the sketchboard as a way of showing their explanation, and then proceed with the investigation.

5. Share after-investigation views.

6. With a partner, draw a series of sketches on a card strip that explains what happened, for example, why needles float or sink.

7. Students use their sketches to share and discuss their explanations.

8. If necessary they modify sketches, and then add a written explanation below each sketch.

For a complex investigation, students might produce a series of sketches explaining why or how something happened at each stage of the investigation. Encourage students to successively modify their sketches.

Note that it might be useful to involve students in the construction of storyboards as part of a video presentation when introducing the How and Why Sketchboard as a prewriting strategy. Alternatively, asking students to reconstruct cut-up comic strips may help them appreciate the causal links between each frame in the cartoon.

How and Why Sketchboard

WHY A BALLOON RISES

• Air heated by flame to about 100°C.

• As air warms, the bits spread out.

• Air inside the balloon is lighter (less dense).

• About $\frac{1}{4}$ of the air goes out the bottom.

• The weight of the balloon is less than the upthrust.

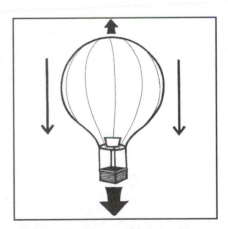

• Air in balloon cools; air comes back in and it sinks.

43

Writing an Explanation

WHAT CAUSES EARTHQUAKES?

THE PHENOMENON (This is the thing you are going to explain)

When the Earth moves suddenly, you may feel an earthquake. But how does this happen? The Earth's crust is made up of huge tectonic plates that all move slowly. Some are pulling apart, others are sliding past each other and some colliding and pushing up mountains. Most earthquakes occur along the boundaries of these plates.

Explanation

In fact, earthquakes are caused by the movement of these plates. As the tectonic plates move and collide with each other they put a great strain on the rocks of the Earth's crust. Sometimes the strain between the plates becomes so great that the rocks of the Earth's crust suddenly snap apart and move into new positions. When that happens, the energy released sends a shock wave for long distances through the rocks causing the ground to shudder and shake, and sometimes tear apart.

Explanation

When the ground tears apart a fault is formed, and once there is a fault in the Earth's crust, movement can go on happening along the fault line in the form of earthquakes. The rocks on either side of the fault are rough so they don't slip past each other smoothly. There is a lot of friction between these rocks and for movement to take place the strain must build up until it is released in the form of an earthquake.

Summary

This is how we think earthquakes occur, but there is more to find out.

Writing an Explanation

An Explanation tells us how something works, or reasons why something happens.

"How" Explanations include:

- How steam engines work.
- How gears work.
- How caterpillars turn into butterflies.
- How calculators work.

"Why" Explanations include:

- Why apples go rotten.
- Why cork floats.
- Why we have tides.
- Why people get angry.

The title of my Explanation is:

_____

Paragraph One

- Say something general about the thing you are going to explain. Decide whether you are writing a "How" or "Why" Explanation.

_____
_____
_____
_____
_____
_____
_____
_____
_____
_____
_____

EXPLANATION
Draft Writing
Framework Model

Writing an Explanation

Paragraph Two

- Write how or why something happens. Use the present tense. You will probably need to use the words **are** and **is** in your sentences. If you are explaining "why" something happens you might write:

    "This is caused by...", "This is due to...", "Because...", "As a result...".

- If you are explaining "how" something works you can write:
    "First...", "Next...", and so on.

_____

_____

_____

_____

_____

_____

_____

_____

_____

_____

_____

Summary Paragraph

- Tell the reader again the thing you have explained. You might begin with: **"This is why...", "This is how...".**

_____

_____

_____

_____

_____

_____

_____

Argument

How to Use a
Creative Problem Solving Framework

Creative Problem Solving helps students to generate and evaluate solutions to problems faced by fictional and historical characters. For example, as the model demonstrates, students might generate creative solutions to a fictional character's problems. Equally, they might generate solutions related to a nation's financial, environmental, or racial problems.

▪ *Students generate solutions.*

The first step in using Creative Problem Solving is to determine a problem central to the text. This is easy with narratives because they have (essentially) a problem-solution structure (the main character has a problem he or she seeks to resolve). Similarly, Creative Problem Solving can be used to think about most historical events. With a little imagination many other situations can be seen in a problem-solution light, for example, animals seeking food and protection, and unstable chemicals seeking to combine with other chemicals. When reading aloud with students, or when students are involved in independent reading, teachers might provide them with a purpose for reading by stating the main problem in the form of a question, as suggested by the model on the following page.

▪ *Many situations can be seen in a problem-solving light.*

Next, students list all their solutions to the problem across the top, then evaluate each one, and record these down the left side. In the Red Riding Hood example, the solution of putting out food has one advantage in that the wolf's life would be spared. The solution of killing the wolf would be cheap. When each solution has been evaluated and recorded, students are ready to use the rating scale. For example, putting out food would save the wolf's life, but in the long run it would not be cheap. Students are then in a strong position to write their Arguments. Again, students might complete the framework in groups then discuss their thinking with other groups. Solutions might be ranked from "excellent" to "failure" and form the basis for discussion and the writing of a transactional text.

▪ *Solutions are discussed in groups.*

Note: The various components of an Argument might be modelled to students progressively over several lessons. Practice with each component could precede the introduction of the next component. The sequence teachers might use when introducing each component is illustrated in the three Argument frameworks later in this book, with the final framework designed to assist students write a complex Argument.

Creative Problem Solving

Problem: In the story of Little Red Riding Hood, how might we stop the wolf from attacking the grandmother?				
Ideas:	Put out food	Kill the wolf	Capture the wolf	Secure granny's house
Evaluation of Ideas:				
Save life	A	F	B	B
Is cheap	F	B	C	C
Quick solution	D	A	B	D
Most humane	A	F	C	B

Our Best Solution(s)

1. If we can afford it, put out food.
2. If we can't afford the food then either capture the wolf or secure Granny's house.

Rating Code

A = Excellent idea

B = Very good idea

C = Average idea

D = Below average idea

F = Total failure

Creative Problem Solving

Problem:				
Ideas:	1.	2.	3.	4.
Evaluation of Ideas:				
1.				
2.				
3.				
4.				

Our Best Solution(s)

_____

_____

_____

_____

Rating Code

A = Excellent idea

B = Very good idea

C = Average idea

D = Below average idea

F = Total failure

49

Writing an Argument

BAN THE AUTOMOBILE

Introduction

Do you like the smell of car exhaust fumes? More and more cars are polluting our cities and some people are saying we need to solve the problem cars create.

Thesis

I believe that people should be banned from owning cars. I believe this for safety, economic, and environmental reasons.

First Reason

First, cars are not safe. This weekend alone, five people were killed on our roads, not to mention the countless unreported number of people involved in non-fatal accidents. People die because they drive.

Second Reason (Alternative)

The second reason why we should ban cars is because they are too expensive. Money spent buying cars would be better spent on more important things like better schools and hospitals. In addition, buying fuel for a car costs a lot of money. Going by bus may not be as convenient but it is cheaper.

Counter Argument

Some people might argue that people need cars. While some people might need a car, many people could walk to work, and others could take public transit.

Restatement

We don't need cars. It makes sense on safety, environmental, and economic grounds to ban cars from our roads.

Writing an Argument: A.

ARGUMENTS CAN BE ONE-SIDED

Title

- The title of my Argument is:

_____

Thesis

Write a paragraph that says what you are arguing for, or against.

- I believe that

_____

_____

_____

_____

- I believe this because

_____

_____

_____

_____

Body

Write a paragraph that says why you believe this.

- First, I believe this because

_____

_____

_____

_____

_____

_____

_____

Writing an Argument: A.

- The second reason is

_____

_____

_____

_____

_____

_____

- Finally I think that

_____

_____

_____

_____

_____

_____

_____

_____

_____

Restatement

Write a paragraph that says, again, what you believe.

- For these reasons I believe that

_____

_____

_____

_____

_____

_____

_____

Writing an Argument: B.

ARGUMENTS CAN LOOK AT MORE THAN ONE SIDE AND SAY WHY THESE ARE WRONG

Title

- The title of my Argument is:

_____

Background

- Write a paragraph that says something about the issue and why people might have a different point of view about it.

_____

_____

_____

_____

Thesis

Write a paragraph that says what you are arguing for, or against.

- I believe that

_____

_____

_____

_____

_____

- I believe this because

_____

_____

_____

_____

_____

ARGUMENT
Draft Writing Framework

Writing an Argument: B.

Body

Write a paragraph that says why you believe this.

- First, I believe this because

  _____

  _____

  _____

  _____

  _____

  _____

  _____

  _____

- The second reason is

  _____

  _____

  _____

  _____

  _____

  _____

  _____

  _____

  _____

- Another reason I believe that

  _____

  _____

  _____

  _____

  _____

  _____

  _____

  _____

Writing an Argument: B.

- Other people believe that

  _____

  _____

  _____

  _____

- But this is wrong because

  _____

  _____

  _____

  _____

- Finally I think that

  _____

  _____

  _____

  _____

  _____

  _____

  _____

Restatement

Write a paragraph that says, again, what you believe.

- For these reasons I believe that

  _____

  _____

  _____

  _____

  _____

  _____

  _____

Writing an Argument: C.

ARGUMENTS CAN BE COMPLEX

Title

- The title of my Argument is:

_____

Background

- Write a paragraph that says something about the issue and why people might have different points of view about it.

_____

_____

_____

_____

_____

_____

Thesis

Write a paragraph that says what you are arguing for, or against.

- I believe that

_____

_____

_____

_____

_____

- I believe this because

_____

_____

_____

_____

_____

_____

Writing an Argument: C.

Body

Write a paragraph that says why you believe this.

- First, I believe this because

_____

_____

_____

_____

_____

_____

_____

- The second reason is

_____

_____

_____

_____

_____

_____

_____

- Another reason I believe that

_____

_____

_____

_____

_____

_____

_____

Writing an Argument: C.

Counter Argument

Write an opposite view, then say what is interesting or worth considering about this view.

- Some people might say that

_____

_____

_____

_____

_____

_____

- Finally I think that

_____

_____

_____

_____

_____

_____

_____

Restatement

Write a paragraph that says, again, what you believe.

- For these reasons I believe that

_____

_____

_____

_____

_____

_____

_____

Discussion

Using the Yes/No Framework

Yes/No Frameworks can be used to think about issues prior to writing Argument and Discussion. Essentially, they assist students to generate, record, and evaluate ideas. Students begin by clearly establishing the issue they wish to think about. This issue might be in the form of an evaluation. For example, "The wolf in Little Red Riding Hood was bad." Alternatively, the issue may be in the form of a prediction. For example, after reading about the potato famine in Ireland, students might predict the consequences across a range of topics including migration, health, and social change.

Alternatively, Yes/No Frameworks could be used to evaluate two hypotheses. For example, a science class might come up with two plausible explanations and need to list their evidence for each hypothesis before reaching a "Best Guess." This should involve students in research prior to and while using the framework.

Students may question the need to complete both sides of a Yes/No Framework prior to writing an Argument. Point out to them that completing the framework will help them choose the strongest side, that is, the side that contains the strongest argument. When students use Argument Framework B they need to understand arguments from both sides so that they can compose counter arguments, usually by choosing the weakest argument from the opposing side. Assist students to compose the debatable statement because this statement gives a purpose for listening, reading, and viewing. Initially, students might complete the Yes/No Frameworks in pairs or groups before using them independently. Again, this signals that students need to thoroughly research a topic before completing the Yes/No Frameworks and encourage them to rehearse their ideas orally, perhaps in the form of a debate, prior to writing.

▌ Students generate, record, and evaluate ideas.

▌ Students weigh evidence.

▌ The Frameworks lead them to choose the strongest argument.

The Yes/No Framework

Write a sentence that says what you want to think about:
That schools should close at lunch time on Fridays.

Reasons Yes	Reasons No
• Students are exhausted by the time Friday comes - they need the rest.	• It might not be possible to fit everything into four and a half days.
• Leaving at lunch time will allow students to start weekend jobs earlier and do homework.	• Young students might not have anyone at home to look after them.
• The teachers will benefit from a shorter day.	• Students might not bother coming in on Friday at all, especially if they have a long way to come.
	• Schools could think of interesting things to do on Friday afternoons to keep students on task.

Conclusion

While there are some advantages to closing early on Friday - there are too many issues related to safety and getting enough work done to weigh in its favor.

The Yes/No Framework

Write a sentence that says what you want to think about:	
Reasons Yes	**Reasons No**
Conclusion	

An alternative structure is presented here.

Write a sentence that says what you want to think about:	
Prediction One	**Prediction Two**
Best Guess	

61

Discussion

Using the Perspective Framework

Perspective Frameworks lead students to think in six complex ways and provide a means of thinking through events, ideas, or issues prior to writing an Argument or Discussion. Apart from the "Talk" perspective they are perhaps best suited to students at upper primary or high school. Even at this level, when used as a conscious prewriting strategy, they should be introduced one at a time. However, this does not prevent teachers using the perspectives to raise the level of thinking when engaged in a class discussion.

- Students are led to think through events, ideas, and issues.

Each perspective serves a different purpose, so perspectives should be selected that suit the event, idea, or issue under consideration. For example, the **Talk** perspective invites students to talk about something from the point of view of animate and inanimate objects. If discussing a train crash, students might talk from the point of view of the train driver, passengers, the train, the owner of the railroad and even the rails that were perhaps bent as a result of an earthquake.

- Talk perspective.

Alternatively, the **Size** perspective might lead students to consider the consequence of something like a fight between two people getting bigger, and eventually ending in a world war. Again, the **Space/Location** perspective may lead students to appreciate the horror of war as if that war was waged over their back fence and not on the other side of the world.

- Size, space, and location perspectives.

The **Culture** perspective helps students appreciate the way different societies might view the same object or event. For example, most Japanese, Norwegians, and Tongans have no problems about hunting whales, while many countries have banned the hunting of whales. Looking at any object or event from different **Angles** provides different perspectives. For example, looking at a whale from above gives you one perspective, but you are hardly likely to appreciate the enormous open mouth unless you see a whale from the front. **Time** changes the way we think about things. What was fine years ago, like the killing of fur seals, might be frowned on today. But in the future, as the colonies of seals grow and fish stocks are depleted, we might think it OK again to kill fur seals.

- Cultural and time perspective.

Each **Conclusion Sentence** on the Framework is designed to lift students' consideration of an immediate event, idea, or issue to some general level that says something about us as humans. For example, discussion using the Talk perspective may result in students concluding that we need to appreciate the points of view of other people. Again, the Space/Location perspective may lead students to conclude that distance dulls our appreciation of events. In short, the Perspective Framework provides ways of thinking through events, ideas, and issues prior to writing, and a way of reaching some big generalizations about the human condition.

Perspective Framework

- **What is the event, idea, or issue you are considering?**

_____

_____

Time:

- What do we think about it today? What will people think about it in the future? What did people think about it in the past?

_____

_____

_____

- Conclusion Sentence

_____

_____

Size:

- If it got much bigger or smaller, would that change the way we think about it?

_____

_____

_____

- Conclusion Sentence

_____

Space/Location:

- What would it look like close up? or from a distance?

_____

_____

_____

- Conclusion Sentence

_____

_____

Perspective Framework

Culture:

- What would the early settlers think about it? What would visitors from another country think about it?

_____

_____

_____

- Conclusion Sentence

_____

_____

Talk:

- If it could talk, what might it say?

_____

_____

_____

- Conclusion Sentence

_____

_____

Angle:

- What does it look like from above? the side? from below?

_____

_____

_____

- Conclusion Sentence

_____

_____

Socratic Questioning

Using the Socratic Questioning Framework

Socratic Questioning is a strategy designed to promote the kind of critical thinking required to write discussions. It is a strategy that assists students to evaluate their own thinking, compare their thinking with others, and consider multiple ideas and the links between and among those ideas.

Students must have a "debatable statement" such as **Whaling Should be Banned** before using the Socratic Questioning Framework. Then, they use the following four questions in turn to discuss the statement.

- **Question One:** Students *consider the source* of their opinion — in short, what evidence leads them to think this way.

- **Question Two:** Students *seek further evidence* supporting their view. Students should be encouraged to provide reasons why they hold a particular view.

- **Question Three:** Students *consider the views* of a person who holds the opposite or a conflicting perspective. For example, what would you say to a person who didn't agree with you? This perspective helps students appreciate other points of view.

- **Question Four:** Students *consider the consequence* of holding a particular opinion — either in support or opposition to the debatable statement. Will the opinion lead to action?

For example, after reading Little Red Riding Hood, the class might conclude "That the wolf was bad". Question One can be answered with:

- the wolf lied to Little Red Riding Hood.

- the wolf attacked Granny.

Question Two can be answered by referring to other books that portray wolves as bad, for example *Peter and the Wolf, The Three Little Pigs,* or news items that recount wolves taking babies.

Question Three prompts students to consider opposing perspectives. For example, the wolf probably doesn't consider himself bad, and an expert on wolves might explain that they are behaving instinctively. There may even be examples of wolves nurturing children.

The final question challenges students to reconsider their opinions, and to take action. For example, if you still believe the wolf is bad you might set about exterminating the species!

▌*Critical thinking is encouraged.*

▌*Students are prompted to see a situation in a variety of ways.*

Socratic Questioning Framework

Debatable Statement

- What I believe is

_____

_____

_____

_____

_____

_____

Question One

- Why do you believe this to be true? Have you always thought this?

_____

_____

_____

_____

_____

_____

Question Two

- Is there support for what you believe?

_____

_____

_____

_____

_____

_____

Socratic Questioning Framework

Question Three

- What would people with the opposite belief say?

_____

_____

_____

_____

_____

_____

Question Four

- What might happen if you continue to hold this belief? What should you do?

_____

_____

_____

_____

_____

_____

SCAMPER Problem Solving

The SCAMPER Problem Solving procedure can be used by students prior to writing Explanation, Argument, Discussion and Report. It provides students with six ways of solving problems.

Procedure

First, students must clearly define the problem. For example, *lead should be banned from gasoline because the lead-filled exhaust causes brain damage.*

Next, in groups, students need to research as they use each way of thinking about the problem.

- The **Substitute** way of problem solving may result in research into aromatics as substitutes for lead, or the use of car pooling as a way of reducing exhaust emissions.

- The **Combine** way of thinking may encourage students to think about the role of chemists, neurologists, and mechanics that might assist in solving the problem.

- Again, **Adapt** and **Modify** may spur students to think of alternate energy sources and the consequences of smog caused by exhaust emissions.

- **Put to other use** might suggest alternative uses for the lead saved from gasoline.

- **Eliminate** might encourage students to consider the positive benefits of reducing lead levels in the atmosphere.

- **Reverse** provides an opportunity for students to consider the consequences of adding even more lead to fuel.

The SCAMPER way of problem solving is likely to benefit students when writing any text that uses a problem/solution text structure. For example, a Report on whales may address the problem of over-hunting, an Explanation of why the ozone layer is depleting may lead to a description of what causes the problem and to ways of halting the depletion. Arguments and Discussions often address problems, and the inclusion of solutions generated using the SCAMPER Problem Solving procedure may strengthen these texts.

This procedure helps students to construct complex discussion texts.

SCAMPER
Problem Solving

- **What is the problem?**

  _____

  _____

  _____

- **Substitute:** What could you use instead? What could you do instead?

  _____

  _____

  _____

  _____

- **Combine:** What could be brought together to solve the problem?

  _____

  _____

  _____

  _____

- **Adapt and Modify:** What could be changed to solve the problem? What would happen if we made something larger, greater, stronger, lighter, or slower?

  _____

  _____

  _____

  _____

SCAMPER Problem Solving

- **Put to other use:** What new ways could we use this problem?

  _____

  _____

  _____

  _____

  _____

  _____

- **Eliminate:** What could we do without?

  _____

  _____

  _____

  _____

  _____

  _____

- **Reverse:** What would you have if you reversed it, turned it
  around, changed the parts or order?

  _____

  _____

  _____

  _____

  _____

  _____

Writing a Discussion

SHOULD WE BAN THE AUTOMOBILE?

Thesis
There are reasons for and against banning people from owning cars.
Discussion Topic One
First, it might be argued that cars are not safe. But if we were to ban something because people might die doing it, we would have to stop using all other forms of transport. There is risk in everything.
Discussion Topic Two
Others might say that we should ban cars because they are too expensive to buy and run; money should be spent on more important things like better schools and hospitals. But this takes away people's freedom to use hard-earned money the way they want to. If they can afford to run a car why should they be forced into a bus?
Discussion Topic Three
The answer to that, some people would say, is that cars should be banned for environmental reasons. Buses carrying 50 people give off less pollution than one gas-fuelled car. But new cars running on unleaded fuel are less of an environmental hazard and some people need cars because it's too far to walk to work and school, and buses are unavailable.
Conclusion
There are good reasons on both sides. Perhaps if we thought more about each other and the planet we share, we might use our cars less — we might all benefit in the end.

Thesis means ...
The Thesis is where you say what you are going to discuss.
The thesis is the "problem".

Writing a Discussion: A.

A DISCUSSION IS A TWO-SIDED ARGUMENT

- **The title of my Discussion is**

_____

Thesis

Write a paragraph saying what you are arguing for and against.

- Some people believe that

_____

_____

_____

_____

- On the other hand, other people believe that

_____

_____

_____

_____

Body

Write paragraphs in the Body of your Discussion that give both sides of the argument.

- First, some people believe that

_____

_____

_____

_____

_____

_____

Writing a Discussion: A.

- A second argument put forward by some people is that

_____

_____

_____

_____

_____

_____

- People opposed to that view say that

_____

_____

_____

_____

_____

_____

Conclusion

Write a paragraph that shows you have thought about both sides.
You might decide who has the stronger case, but you might like to
just provide a brief summary of the main points made by each side.

_____

_____

_____

_____

_____

_____

_____

_____

Writing a Discussion: B.

A DISCUSSION CAN BE DETAILED

- **The title of my Discussion is**

_____

Thesis

Write a paragraph saying what you are arguing for and against.

- Some people believe that

_____

_____

_____

_____

- On the other hand, other people believe that

_____

_____

_____

_____

Body

Write paragraphs in the Body of your Discussion that give both sides of the argument.

- First, some people believe that

_____

_____

_____

_____

_____

_____

_____

_____

DISCUSSION

Draft Writing Framework

Writing a Discussion: B.

- A second argument put forward by some people is that

_____
_____
_____
_____
_____
_____

- On the other hand others say that

_____
_____
_____
_____
_____
_____
_____

- Another argument put forward by some people is that

_____
_____
_____
_____
_____
_____
_____
_____

75

Writing a Discussion: B.

- People opposed to that view say that

_____

_____

_____

_____

_____

_____

_____

- Most people agree that

_____

_____

_____

_____

_____

_____

_____

_____

_____

- But there are still some people who suggest that

_____

_____

_____

_____

_____

_____

_____

Writing a Discussion: B.

Conclusion

Write a paragraph that shows you have thought about both sides.
You might decide who has the stronger case, but you might like to
just provide a brief summary of the main points made by each side.

_____

_____

_____

_____

_____

_____

_____

_____

Assessing Writing

How to Use
The Writing Record Form

The record form is in two sections:

- **Section One** provides descriptors against which teachers might assess the general strategies students use while writing, and the general qualities of students' writing.

- **Section Two** provides descriptors against which the use of prewriting strategies and the conventions of each form of factual writing might be assessed.

The descriptors in Section One can be used to assess any form of writing, but the descriptors in Section Two are specific to the genres described in this resource.

The assessment is recorded on an arrow that indicates the degree of independence students exhibit in their use of strategies, and the inclusion of various qualities in the writing. This record system provides the teacher with flexibility in the way they rate students. It also accommodates the fluctuating nature of the learning process — students may exhibit independence one day and more dependence the next. The system is consistent with empowering writers rather than comparing their performance.

Teachers will probably want to select the sections of the record form that suit their program and create a folder for each student. Some additional information will be entered during conferences with the student, other information entered after the sensitive observation of students' writing behavior in class.

ASSESSMENT

Writing Record Form

SECTION ONE

Name:

Class: Dates:

General Prewriting Strategies

Decides on purpose   DEPENDENT ←——————————————→ INDEPENDENT

Selects appropriate genre   DEPENDENT ←——————————————→ INDEPENDENT

Determines audience   DEPENDENT ←——————————————→ INDEPENDENT

General Writing Strategies

Writes on every second line   DEPENDENT ←——————————————→ INDEPENDENT

Deletes words   DEPENDENT ←——————————————→ INDEPENDENT

Inserts words   DEPENDENT ←——————————————→ INDEPENDENT

Relocates words   DEPENDENT ←——————————————→ INDEPENDENT

Uses invented spelling   DEPENDENT ←——————————————→ INDEPENDENT

Uses peer conferences   DEPENDENT ←——————————————→ INDEPENDENT

Reads work aloud   DEPENDENT ←——————————————→ INDEPENDENT

Shapes work appropriately   DEPENDENT ←——————————————→ INDEPENDENT

General Post Writing Strategies

Responds to writing   DEPENDENT ←——————————————→ INDEPENDENT

Identifies something they like   DEPENDENT ←——————————————→ INDEPENDENT

Asks questions   DEPENDENT ←——————————————→ INDEPENDENT

Identifies something to change   DEPENDENT ←——————————————→ INDEPENDENT

Acts on advice   DEPENDENT ←——————————————→ INDEPENDENT

General Qualities

Enough information   DEPENDENT ←——————————————→ INDEPENDENT

Clearly expressed   DEPENDENT ←——————————————→ INDEPENDENT

Coherent   DEPENDENT ←——————————————→ INDEPENDENT

Keeps to topic   DEPENDENT ←——————————————→ INDEPENDENT

Has voice   DEPENDENT ←——————————————→ INDEPENDENT

Achieves purpose   DEPENDENT ←——————————————→ INDEPENDENT

Appropriate vocabulary   DEPENDENT ←——————————————→ INDEPENDENT

Writing Record Form

SECTION TWO

RECOUNT

Prewriting Strategies

timeline

Draws timeline   DEPENDENT ←————————————→ INDEPENDENT

Labels timeline   DEPENDENT ←————————————→ INDEPENDENT

sequencing

Draws pictures   DEPENDENT ←————————————→ INDEPENDENT

Sequences pictures   DEPENDENT ←————————————→ INDEPENDENT

Captions pictures   DEPENDENT ←————————————→ INDEPENDENT

Writes link words   DEPENDENT ←————————————→ INDEPENDENT

General Characteristics

Time ordered   DEPENDENT ←————————————→ INDEPENDENT

Past tense   DEPENDENT ←————————————→ INDEPENDENT

Paragraphs   DEPENDENT ←————————————→ INDEPENDENT

PROCEDURE

Prewriting Strategies

Flow Chart Framework   DEPENDENT ←————————————→ INDEPENDENT

General Characteristics

Event sequenced   DEPENDENT ←————————————→ INDEPENDENT

Present tense   DEPENDENT ←————————————→ INDEPENDENT

DESCRIPTION

Prewriting Strategies

Observational drawing   DEPENDENT ←————————————→ INDEPENDENT

Record Sheet   DEPENDENT ←————————————→ INDEPENDENT

Writing Record Form

General Characteristics

Topical   DEPENDENT ←——————————————————→ INDEPENDENT

Present tense   DEPENDENT ←——————————————————→ INDEPENDENT

Paragraphs   DEPENDENT ←——————————————————→ INDEPENDENT

REPORT

Prewriting Strategies

brainstorm

Collects words   DEPENDENT ←——————————————————→ INDEPENDENT

Groups words   DEPENDENT ←——————————————————→ INDEPENDENT

Labels groups   DEPENDENT ←——————————————————→ INDEPENDENT

Designs questions   DEPENDENT ←——————————————————→ INDEPENDENT

Identifies resources   DEPENDENT ←——————————————————→ INDEPENDENT

characteristics grid

Completes prep'd grid   DEPENDENT ←——————————————————→ INDEPENDENT

Completes part'l grid   DEPENDENT ←——————————————————→ INDEPENDENT

Designs own grid   DEPENDENT ←——————————————————→ INDEPENDENT

Writes summaries   DEPENDENT ←——————————————————→ INDEPENDENT

General Characteristics

General classification   DEPENDENT ←——————————————————→ INDEPENDENT

Subheadings   DEPENDENT ←——————————————————→ INDEPENDENT

Topical paragraphs   DEPENDENT ←——————————————————→ INDEPENDENT

Present tense   DEPENDENT ←——————————————————→ INDEPENDENT

Writing Record Form

EXPLANATION

Prewriting Strategies

How and Why Framework   DEPENDENT ←——————————————→ INDEPENDENT

General Characteristics

Phenomenon   DEPENDENT ←——————————————→ INDEPENDENT

Explanation   DEPENDENT ←——————————————→ INDEPENDENT

Summary   DEPENDENT ←——————————————→ INDEPENDENT

Present tense   DEPENDENT ←——————————————→ INDEPENDENT

ARGUMENT AND DISCUSSION

Prewriting Strategies

yes/no framework

Designs statement   DEPENDENT ←——————————————→ INDEPENDENT

Completes web   DEPENDENT ←——————————————→ INDEPENDENT

Writes conclusion   DEPENDENT ←——————————————→ INDEPENDENT

perspective framework

Talk   DEPENDENT ←——————————————→ INDEPENDENT

Time   DEPENDENT ←——————————————→ INDEPENDENT

Size   DEPENDENT ←——————————————→ INDEPENDENT

Space   DEPENDENT ←——————————————→ INDEPENDENT

Culture   DEPENDENT ←——————————————→ INDEPENDENT

Location   DEPENDENT ←——————————————→ INDEPENDENT

General Characteristics

Background   DEPENDENT ←——————————————→ INDEPENDENT

Thesis   DEPENDENT ←——————————————→ INDEPENDENT

Body   DEPENDENT ←——————————————→ INDEPENDENT

Restatement   DEPENDENT ←——————————————→ INDEPENDENT

Present tense   DEPENDENT ←——————————————→ INDEPENDENT

Index